DIE LAUGHING

BY
LAWRENCE KANE
MURRAY STEIN
KRISTI KANE

Illustrations by Alex Tavoularis

A DOLPHIN BOOK
DOUBLEDAY & COMPANY, INC.
GARDEN CITY, NEW YORK
1980

Printed in the United States of America
Library of Congress Catalog Card Number 79-7498
ISBN: 0-385-15071-7

9 8 7 6 5 4 3 2

PREFACE

How did this crazy idea of having fun with tombstones come into being? Who is the macabre cad who could have dreamed up this unsanctimonious treatment of poor souls—some of whom have long passed away—even some who are still with us—and others who are merely fictional and never lived at all?

My daughter, Kristi, that's who. I'll get back to telling you how it all happened, but first let me put you at ease if you think the subject matter herein contained is irreverent.

Did you ever stop to think about how come the word "funeral" starts with the word "fun"? Never occurred to you, right? Why, you may now ask, should such a solemn, lugubrious rite have the word "fun" associated with it?

Going back in time, the word "funeral" was probably arrived at by a combination of the words "fun" and "eral." Fun meant just what it means today, namely fun, and "eral," as everyone knows, means of the particular historical period. So then, we have "funeral" meaning fun of the historical period of that particular time. This came about because in actuality there was little to do during that distant past, other than stare up at the sky or listen to the grass grow. It was only when someone "passed on" that some real activity was generated. Usually a celebration, accompanied by revelry for several days, to perpetuate the memory of the deceased and to blow the minds of the living. If you've ever been to a good old-fashioned wake, or one of those "Saints Go Marching In" type of funerals with all that jazz, you would realize that while there is tragedy in death there is also a need for a diversion—to halt the tears and sorrow and to speed the departed happily on his or her way.

Perhaps the American Indians said it best by describing the deceased as heading for the "Happy Hunting Grounds." I don't know what we're all going to be hunting for up there, but as long as we're going to be happy doing it, who cares? Now that I have logically explained the "fun" approach to this classic you are about to browse through, let me get back to my daughter, Kristi, who I left standing in paragraph two.

Kristi is a crossword puzzle freak—as are her mother, father, three sisters, and brother. The New York *Times* Sunday magazine section, which contains those great crosswords, was always the most fought-after item in our household each week. The first one to awaken would rush out to the end of the long driveway of our home in suburbia, in foul weather or fair, to be first to pick up the paper as soon as it was delivered, in order to have first crack at the puzzle. It was subsequently erased so the next one could get his or her turn at it.

Then, one Sunday it was announced in the New York *Times* that Will Weng, the longtime editor of the *Times* crossword puzzle, was going into retirement. How sad when we all learned of this. How great was Will Weng. How many hundreds of happy hours he had given all of us in the Kane family—and I'm sure millions of other crossword freaks everywhere.

Since to a gal Kristi's age (now twenty-six) retirement means one foot in the grave, she came to me with this crazy notion and the accompanying drawing. "Dad, when Will Weng dies, I think his tombstone will probably read like this":

I thought this was kind of a cute notion, especially when she came back to me a day or so later and said, "I've got an even better one for Will Weng," and proceeded to show me this:

Murray Stein, an art director and close acquaintance, flipped over the concept. It was with his diligence and perseverance that *Die Laughing* got off the ground. Murray set the wheels in motion by sketching the ones we dreamed up and added many of his own along the way.

Since an advertising person does not go all out with a concept until it is "market tested," I showed the project to a panel of expert, my wife. She approved, and she's a tough critic. When we approached Doubleday, the reception was warm and favorable and here we are. It's all here for you to have fun with. Some of the concepts are not so obvious, and you may have to study them a while if you feel you're not getting the point. They are all somewhat cerebral and call for general knowledge and, to a degree, some truck with trivia. If you can't figure some of them out, ask an egghead friend to explain.

That's about all I'm going to tell you. Have fun, and get a copy for every friend you have who has a sense of humor and a bit of gray matter to meet some of the cerebral challenges.

Lawrence Kane

One more word...

After you've gotten the hang of *Die Laughing*, and if you think these tombstones are fun and easy to do, we offer you a challenge and a reward. Think up your own and mail it, or them, in. We'll pay $25 in cold hard cash for every entry we use in *Die Laughing*, Volume II, and we'll give you a credit line, too. Entries are non-returnable. In the event two or more similar ideas are submitted by different folks, the earliest postmark will determine the victor.

You don't have to be an artist, just send in your concept with a rough sketch, that's all. Mail it to *Die Laughing*, c/o Doubleday & Company, Inc., 245 Park Avenue, New York, New York 10017.

The Authors

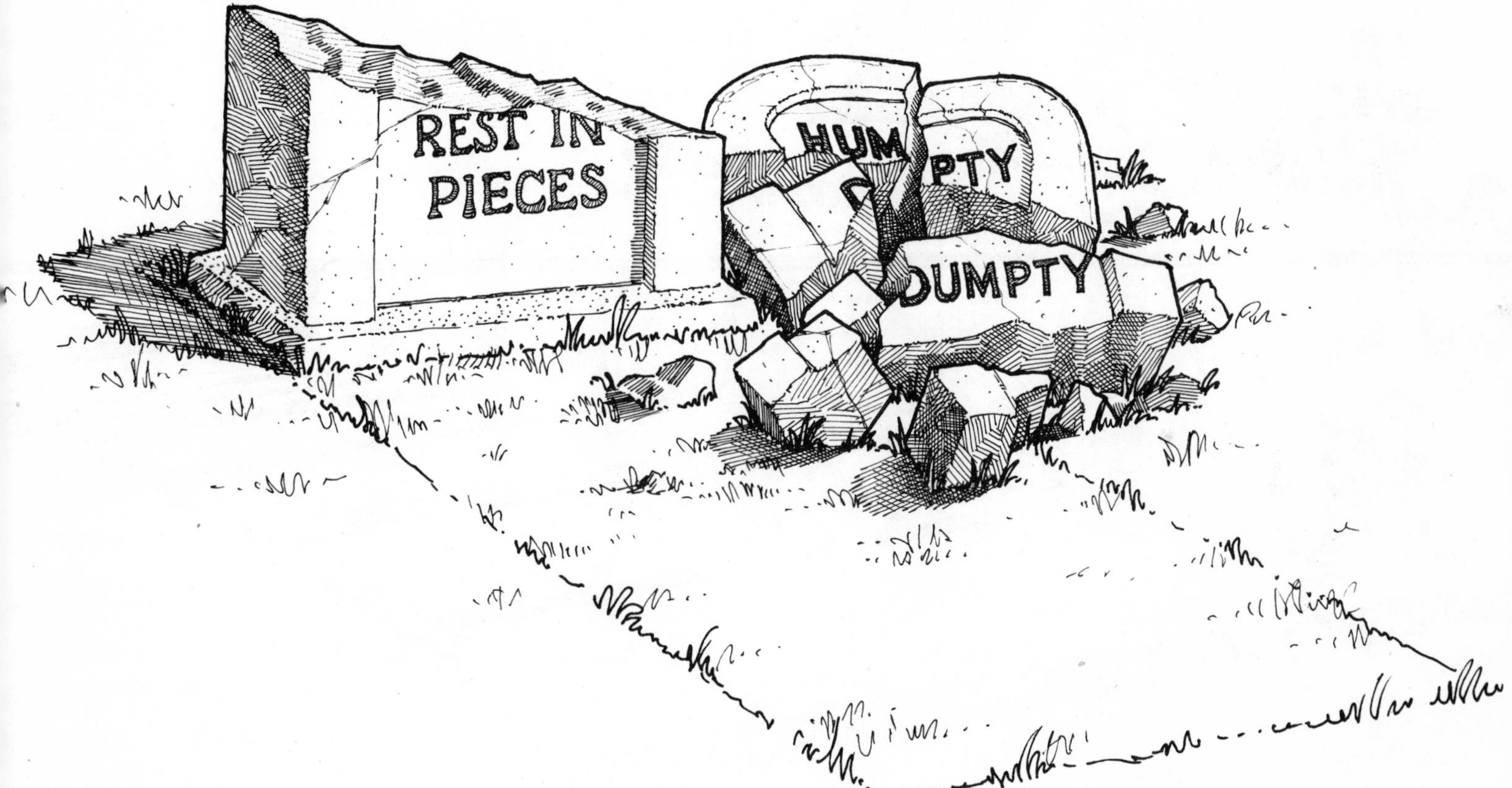
REST IN
PIECES
HUMPTY
DUMPTY

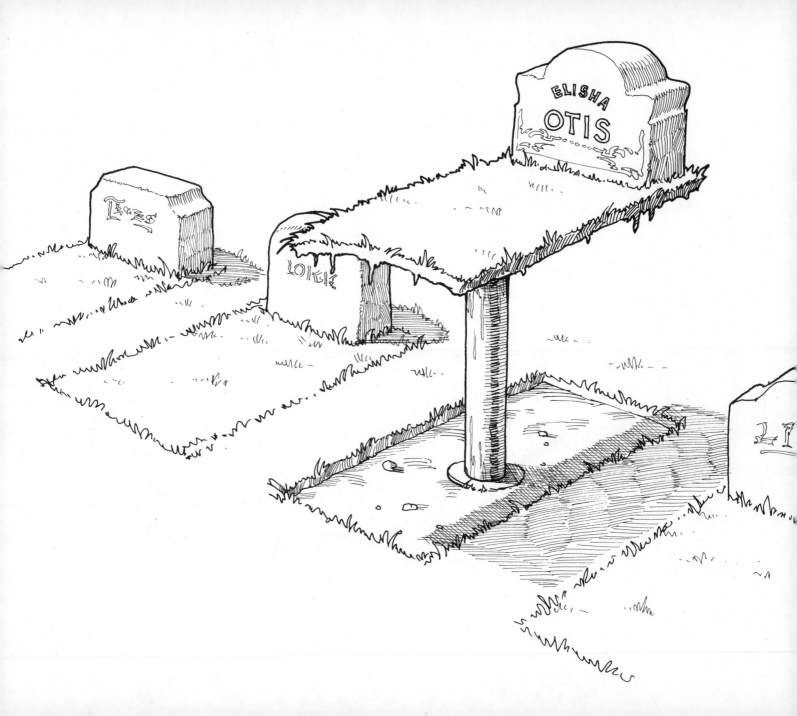

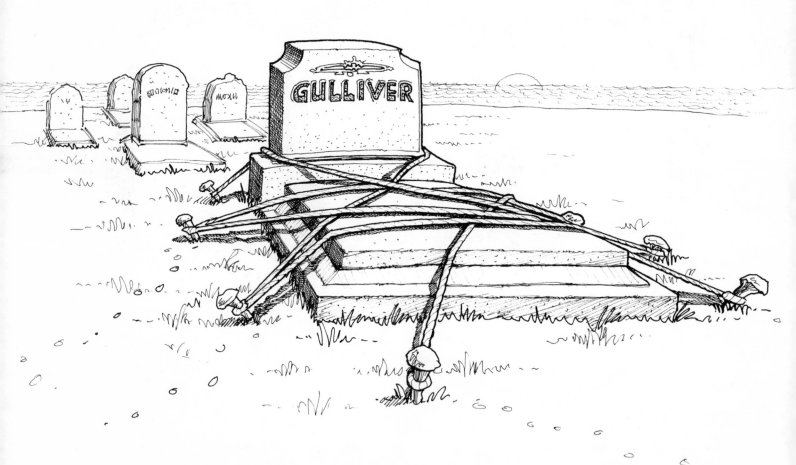